The Digestive System

Ben Morrison

the rosen publishing group's
rosen central

Published in 2001 by The Rosen Publishing Group, Inc.
29 East 21st Street, New York, NY 10010

Copyright © 2001 by The Rosen Publishing Group, Inc.

First Edition

Library of Congress Cataloging in Publication Data

Morrison, Ben.
    Insider's guide to the body: the digestive system / By Ben Morrison. — 1st ed.
        p.   cm. — (Insider's guide to the body)
    ISBN 0-8239-3337-7
  1. Gastrointestinal system—Juvenile literature. [1. Digestive system.] I. Title. II. Series.
    QP145 .M674 2000
    612.3—dc21

00-010324

Manufactured in the United States of America

Contents

1   What Is the Digestive System?   4

2   A Trip from the Mouth
    to the Stomach   6

3   The Regulatory and Absorption
    Centers in Digestion   16

4   The Wonderful World of Waste   24

5   Digestive Health   34

    Glossary   42
    For More Information   43
    For Further Reading   45
    Index   46

1
What is the Digestive System?

You might not be thinking about it, but your digestive system is probably working right now. Did you have breakfast this morning? Did you or will you have lunch this afternoon or dinner this evening? Every time you eat, your digestive system starts working.

Your digestive system is the system of organs that processes the food you eat and breaks it down into the nutrients that your body needs to function and grow.

What Does "Digestion" Mean?

The word "digestion" has a Latin root, *digerere*, which means "to arrange." If you think about it, that is exactly what the digestive system does: It breaks down the food you eat and arranges the various components into parts that your body can use.

Digestion starts with chewing and ends when you go to the bathroom. In between those times the digestive system is working—

breaking up the food, sorting out the nutrients that your body needs, and preparing the leftover waste to be excreted (removed from the body) when you go to the bathroom. The circulatory system uses your blood to transport the nutrients throughout your body, bringing necessary materials to all your cells.

More than any other system in your body, the digestive system can be seen as a kind of factory or power plant. Materials (food) go in and energy (sugars), usable products (the proteins and fats that your body uses to repair itself and grow), and waste come out. To do all of this takes several different organs with specific— and not-so-specific—functions. These organs are regulated by your nervous system and by various hormones in your body.

You can also think of your digestive system as a large tube. The technical name for this tube is the gastrointestinal tract. The tube, or tract, of the human digestive system stretches twenty-five to thirty-five feet. If you think that's long, imagine how long it would be if you spread it out: If you were to unfold all of the folds and crevices of the human digestive system into one flat surface, you would find that the surface area of the human digestive system is roughly as big as a tennis court.

2

A Trip from the Mouth to the Stomach

Although you probably don't think about your digestive system often, there is something related to it that you think about every day: food. Your day is framed around when you eat. When you eat is mostly determined by routine. If you eat every day at a certain hour, then your body conditions itself to expect food at that hour. If you go without food when your body expects it, you become hungry. Your feeling of hunger is controlled by the hunger center in your brain, located near the hypothalamus. Your hunger center is triggered not only by routine but also by outside stimuli (things you hear, smell, see, or touch), such as the smell of good food cooking.

Before You Eat: What and When You Eat

What you think of as "good food" and what you prefer to eat is determined by a variety of factors. Some of the most important factors are culture and custom—where you live and what your lifestyle is like. But

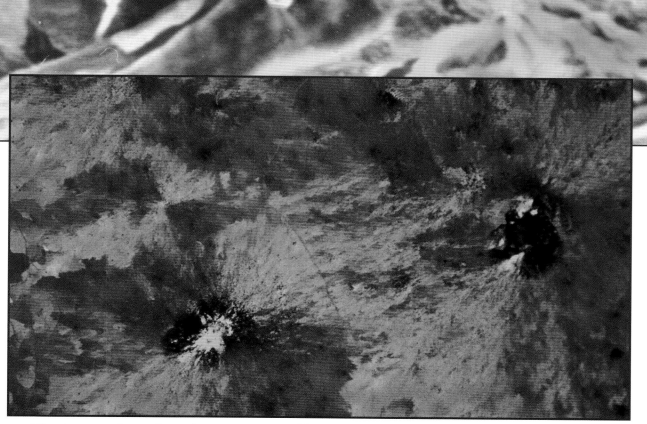

The image above is a close-up view of human taste buds. The tongue not only enables us to taste food but also aids in the process of chewing.

even though cultural differences between people are wide and varied, people's diets consist of the same basic items: proteins, carbohydrates, fats, vitamins, and minerals. For example, in some cultures people get their daily allowance of complex carbohydrates (also known as starches) from bread, in others, from noodles, and in still others, from rice. Proteins are an even better example. In some cultures, people get their proteins from diets heavy in meat or fish, while in others, people don't eat meat at all, and get their protein in other ways.

Proteins and carbohydrates make up the bulk of what we eat. Carbohydrates are either sugars (known as simple carbohydrates) or starches (known as complex carbohydrates) and are broken down by the digestive system into simple sugars that the body's cells use for energy.

Proteins are the body's building blocks. One job of the digestive system is to break down proteins into their basic components, called

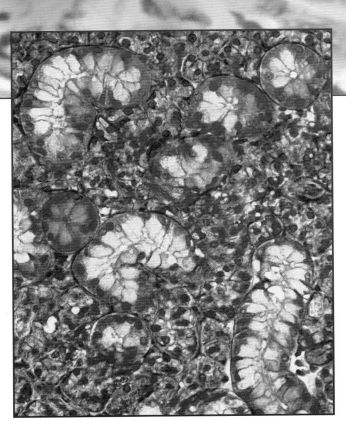

This is a magnification of a salivary gland. Your salivary glands secrete saliva which plays a key role in the process of chewing your food.

amino acids. There are twenty-six amino acids, each of which is needed by the body's cells. In addition to proteins and carbohydrates, the body needs fat, vitamins, and minerals, but not in nearly the same amounts.

Now it's time to start eating.

Eating and Chewing

Chewing is the first way that your body begins to digest food. What we call "eating" is the first step of the digestive journey, and of course, your mouth starts it off. All the parts of your mouth—the tongue, salivary glands, and the teeth—have their own specific function in chewing. Chewing is a process accomplished by your teeth, but also involves your tongue and your spit, more properly called saliva. As you know, chewing is over once you swallow.

When food enters your mouth it has to go through your teeth. Your teeth are specialized to do certain things to break down food. The teeth toward the front of your mouth are called incisors. Their job is to bite off the food you eat into small (bite-sized) chunks.

You also have pointy teeth called canines. These teeth are much more prominent in hunting animals, such as dogs and cats—who use

Different kinds of teeth help to break down your food in different ways.

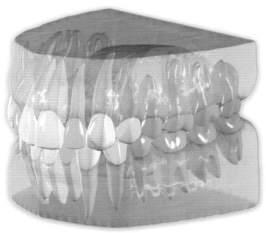

their canines for holding their prey—than in humans. Human canines help by tearing the food apart.

Finally, you have your molars and premolars. Your molars and premolars are the thick teeth at the back of your mouth that mash food. Working together, the jaw muscles of an adult can exert 200 pounds of pressure on the molars, which is enough to break down very tough meats.

As you chew, the tongue moves the food around the mouth from the incisors to the molars so that all of your teeth can do their job. Teeth, tongue, and jaw muscles can't accomplish the task of chewing alone, however. Saliva, which is secreted from your salivary glands in the back of your mouth, is a very important part of the process.

In fact, you can't even taste food without saliva. Try this: Start by eating a large piece of bread. When you place the bread in your mouth, it will start out as a lump without any taste at all. As you chew, it will taste somewhat sweeter. This is because of an enzyme called amylase, which is present in your saliva. When amylase interacts with the bread, it breaks down the bread into basic sugar and starches.

Moving Along: The Esophagus

Chewing and eating are voluntary acts; we have control over them. Whether we think about it or not, we can change how

SECRETS OF GOOD TASTE: THE HUMAN TONGUE

The human tongue has about nine thousand taste buds, and different taste buds in different sections of the tongue pick up on different types of taste. For example, the taste buds at the front of the tongue taste sweet substances, while the taste buds at the back taste bitter things. Taste is one way the human body protects itself from eating harmful things. For example, extremely repulsive tastes, such as strong bitterness, can indicate poisons.

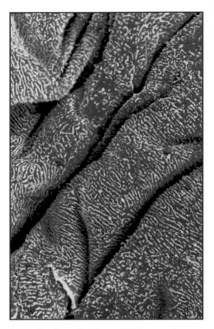

Taste buds in different sections of the tongue pick up different tastes.

well we chew and how quickly we eat by controlling the various muscles involved.

At this stage, when the food is turned into a liquefied ball in your mouth, it is called a bolus. When you swallow, the tongue pushes the bolus past the cavity in the back of your mouth, called the pharynx. In all, twenty-two separate muscle groups are necessary for swallowing. One of those muscle groups in the back of the mouth controls the valve called the epiglottis. The epiglottis covers the windpipe, also called the trachea, and allows the bolus to pass into the food pipe, or the esophagus.

After swallowing the bolus (the term for chewed food), however, everything that happens until the excretion stage (that is, when you go to the bathroom), is involuntary: The body handles it by itself. This

includes the muscle contractions known as peristalsis.

Peristalsis is the technical term for the muscle contractions in the esophagus. These contractions create a wave-like motion that push the food down. Peristalsis is similar to holding a bar of soap in your hand. If you squeeze one end, you push the soap out of your hand. Similarly, peristalsis works by contracting the muscles above the bolus while easing up the muscles below it.

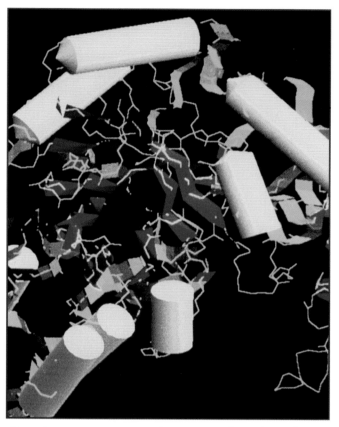

Amylase, an enzyme in your saliva, breaks down food, enabling you to taste it.

If you think that gravity pushes the food down, you're wrong. You can actually eat upside down and peristalsis will push the food up (or is that down?) into your stomach.

Peristalsis pushes the food through the esophagus and into the stomach. The esophagus is about ten inches long, and to travel the length of the esophagus takes the bolus about six seconds for well-chewed food and up to several minutes for dryer, ill-chewed food (your parents tell you to chew carefully for a reason!).

At the bottom of the esophagus is a valve called the cardiac, or esophageal, sphincter. A sphincter is the technical term for a ring of

The image above is an electron micrograph (magnification x720) of the mucous membrane lining the stomach. The hole at the center is the entrance to a gastric gland.

muscle that controls an opening, and the digestive system has many of them. When the esophageal sphincter isn't working correctly, it can let acids from the stomach escape into the esophagus. Although this process has nothing to do with the heart, it is called heartburn. (You can read more about this in chapter 4.)

Breaking It Down: The Stomach

After passing through the esophagus, the bolus enters the stomach. The stomach is a small J-shaped sac where most of the process of digestion takes place. Although you might point to your belly button to signify your stomach, your stomach is actually higher up—it's just below your heart, inside your ribcage.

When you are not eating, the stomach looks like a deflated balloon, and is anywhere from eight to ten inches long. Luckily, when you eat heartily, it can expand to hold up to seven pints of food and liquid. That's almost the equivalent of a full gallon.

The stomach's main job is to digest all the types of food that enter your stomach. This can be quite a job if you consider the wide variety of foods you probably eat. A bolus may be hard or soft, acidic or alkaline, watery or solid—the stomach has to digest it, no matter what.

Food usually stays in the stomach for about three to five hours. An excessive amount of fat in the bolus increases the amount of time that it spends in the stomach. After the stomach has done its work, what's left of the food is no longer called a bolus. It has become a yellowish liquid called chyme.

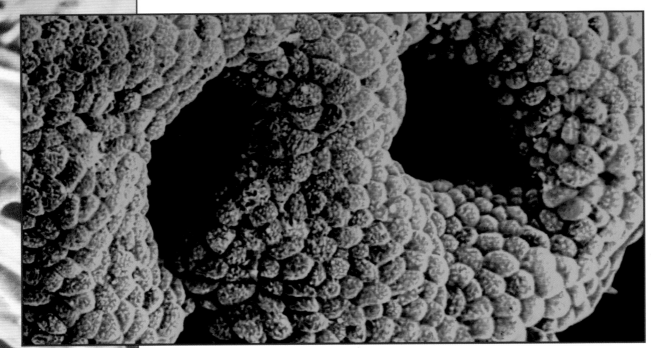

Hydrochloric acid aids in digesting complex proteins and killing bacteria. It is secreted by gastric glands which open into the stomach through gastric pits (the dark holes above).

Much like the way salivary glands produce amylase, the stomach produces its own enzymes to help break down food. The enzymes in the stomach are much more powerful and varied than those in saliva, however. The first is called pepsin. Pepsin breaks down proteins into less complex components called peptides and polypeptides. These will be broken down into even smaller pieces, called amino acids, later on. Another enzyme in the stomach is lipase, which works on some fats to break them down into fatty acids and glycerol.

The final substance used by the stomach is hydrochloric acid. Hydrochloric acid is an extremely strong acid that acts along with pepsin to digest complex proteins. Hydrochloric acid also kills a good deal of the bacteria that might try to invade the body.

One of the reasons we know what we do about the digestive system is because of an amazing hole or "window" into the stomach of Alexis St. Martin. In 1822, St. Martin, a young Canadian trapper, was shot at close range in his left side. The bullet went into his stomach. St. Martin was treated by a U.S. Army doctor named William Beaumont. Beaumont treated St. Martin with success, but was unable to close the wound completely. What happened next is pretty amazing: Beaumont was able, through the hole, to observe what happened in St. Martin's stomach when foods were eaten. Beaumont could also watch what happened when St. Martin experienced various emotions. Beaumont studied the hole into St. Martin for eight years.

To do all of this, hydrochloric acid has to be quite powerful. In fact, it is stronger than the battery acid in a car battery, and if you were to pour it on a wooden table, it would dissolve right through the table. Luckily, the stomach has a protective layer of mucus, an almost liquid-like protective surface that stops the hydrochloric acid from eating the stomach itself. (When the lining fails to do this, you may develop an ulcer. Check out chapter 4 for more details.)

Although the primary function of the stomach is this form of basic digestion, some substances, such as alcohol, aspirin, and water, begin to be absorbed into the bloodstream while in the stomach. But absorption really begins when the chyme moves past the stomach opening, called the pyloric sphincter, and into the next section of the digestive system. Read on to follow that food.

3

The Regulatory and Absorption Centers in Digestion

Digestion is not simply the process of breaking down food; digestion is as much a process of filtering out the poisons, or toxins, that might enter the body and of absorbing nutrients into the bloodstream. In this chapter, we will examine the biliary system and the organs within it—the small intestine and the liver—that perform these more specialized digestive functions.

These organs, especially the liver and the small intestine, are closely connected to the circulatory system (the system that sends blood through your body). One of the heart's jobs is to pump blood to and from the digestive system to pick up nutrients that will be used in the body's cells. Blood flows to the areas of the digestive system through the hepatic artery and returns—carrying important nutrients and vitamins—via the hepatic vein.

The Biliary System

Before we continue on with our journey following the food (or the bolus or chyme), we'll take a detour into the biliary system. The

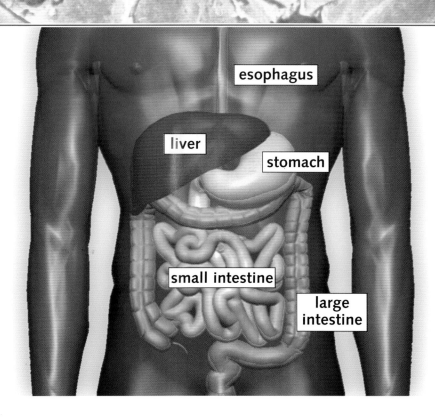

esophagus

liver

stomach

small intestine

large intestine

The liver is the largest organ in the digestive system, and it performs many functions. It produces bile; stores iron, vitamins, and glycogen; and filters toxins from the blood.

biliary system, a support system for the digestive system, is responsible for making bile, a yellow liquid that is about 97 percent water. Its purpose is to break down fats, and it is particularly helpful for digesting especially fatty meals. (We will meet up again with our chyme in the small intestine.)

The Liver

The liver is not really part of the biliary system, but it does produce bile, among other things. The liver is the largest organ in the digestive system. In fact, the liver is the largest internal organ in your entire body. It is about the size of a football, stretching across the width of the body, and it weighs about three pounds.

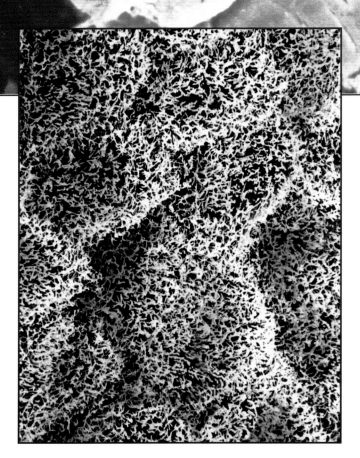

The liver is a very porous organ. More than a quart of blood passes through it every sixty seconds.

The reason that it is so large is because it has to do so many things.

Along with producing bile, the liver acts as a storage facility by storing iron, vitamins, and glycogen. Glycogen is a storable form of glucose, the sugar that the body's cells convert to energy. By storing glucose as glycogen, the liver stores energy for the body to use between meals. Finally, the liver acts as a filtering device by removing poisons from the blood and converting them into safer elements.

The liver's composition aids in all of these functions. The liver is a very porous organ, somewhat like a "sponge" for blood. The liver allows more than a quart of blood—mainly from other parts of the digestive tract, like the small intestine—to pass through every sixty seconds.

The blood passes through canals in the liver called capillaries and into the liver cells known as hepatocytes. Hepatocytes carry out more than 500 functions, but their primary function in digestion is to manufacture bile. The bile created here is secreted through bile ducts into the common hepatic duct and then into the gall bladder, where it is stored.

The pancreas is part of the digestive system and the endocrine system. Its digestive function is to secrete enzymes that break down chyme.

The Gall Bladder

The main function of the gall bladder is to concentrate and store bile. It is a small saclike organ that is located just below the liver. The gall bladder concentrates the bile by removing water from it. (Remember, bile is originally 97 percent water.) The gall bladder releases bile into the first part of the small intestine, called the duodenum, to aid in digestion.

The Pancreas

The pancreas is a long organ located just under the stomach. It is part of both the digestive system and the endocrine system (the system that regulates hormones and has other important functions).

The pancreas, like other components of the digestive system, helps break down chyme. To do this, the pancreas secretes enzymes,

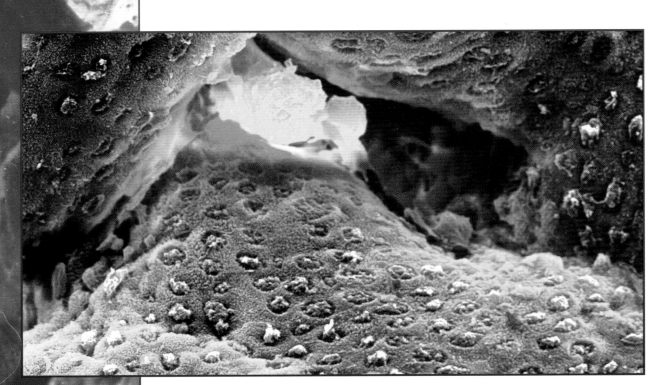

Despite its name, the small intestine can be between fifteen and twenty feet long, providing a large surface area for effective food absorption.

much like the salivary glands and the stomach do. These different enzymes include amylase, which digests starches; lipase, which digests fats; and trypsin, which digests proteins. The other role of the pancreas (as part of the endocrine system) is to regulate the amount of sugar in the blood by producing the hormone insulin, and the amount of acid in the stomach.

The Small Intestine

The pancreas belongs to two different systems, but the small intestine is solely concerned with digestion. When we last saw our chyme, it was being passed through the pyloric sphincter of the stomach into the small intestine. At the same time that the chyme enters the small intestine, bile produced in the liver and stored in the gall bladder, along with enzymes from the pancreas, enter the first part of the small intestine.

The small intestine has three distinct parts: The first is the duodenum (pronounced doo-uh-DEAN-um), the second is the jejunum (je-JU-num), and the third is the ileum (ILL-ee-um). And don't think that the small intestine is so small either; it's more like a coiled hose, and it can be between fifteen and twenty feet long. In comparison, the large intestine is only three to five feet long.

A Frenzy of Enzymes

As we have seen, the digestive system has been preparing the foods we eat to be used by the body's cells. The small intestine continues the process by unleashing a mob of enzymes. In the first part of the intestine, the duodenum, the chyme comes into contact with all of the enzymes made in the pancreas.

Coming from the pancreas, lipase breaks down fats into fatty acids and glucose, the sugar that the body's cells use for energy. Amylase, also from the pancreas, breaks down starch. Trypsin, the third enzyme made in the pancreas, enters the duodenum to break down proteins.

In addition to the enzymes from the pancreas, the small intestine secretes its own enzymes. The small intestine secretes enzymes that break down disaccharides (complex sugars) into monosaccharides (simple sugars). Other enzymes that the small intestine secretes break down peptides, which are broken-down proteins, into amino acids, the most basic components of proteins.

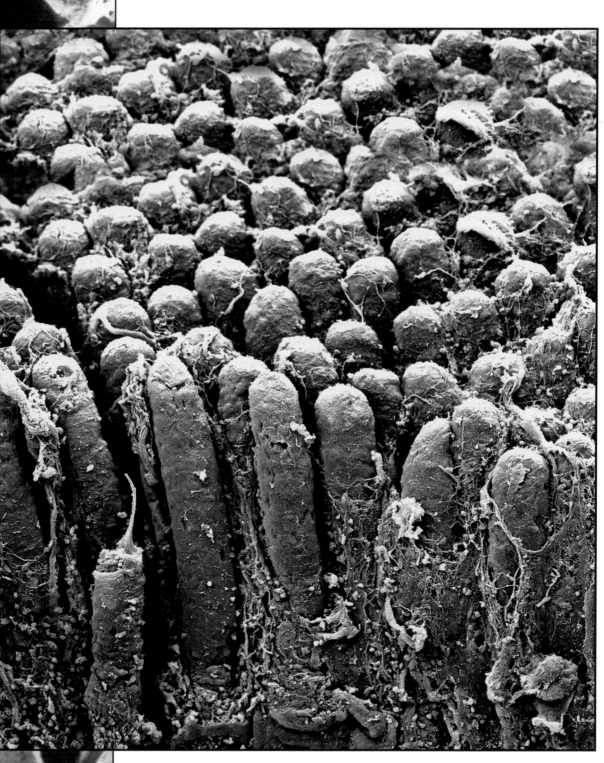

The inside of the duodenum is lined with villi, small fingerlike coils. The walls of the villi allow nutrients to pass into nearby arteries to be distributed throughout the body.

A Quick Pick-Me-Up

The small intestine does more than break down the chyme into nutrients for use in the body. The small intestine is also like a warehouse where those nutrients are picked up by the blood to be distributed throughout the entire body.

The inner part of the small intestine is lined with thousands of small, fingerlike coils known as villi. Villi are less than 1/8 of an inch long. The walls of the villi are specially constructed to allow substances to pass from the small intestine into the nearby arteries, which pick up the nutrients and distribute them to the rest of the body.

Each of the three distinct sections of the small intestine allows for different nutrients to be absorbed by the blood. The first twelve inches of the duodenum provide the blood with most of the vitamins and minerals that will be passed into the body. The duodenum also allows for simple sugars called monosaccharides to be absorbed. Monosaccharides will be used by the body's cells to produce energy. Finally, the duodenum also absorbs fats.

The second part of the small intestine, the jejunum, allows the blood to absorb more complex sugars and vitamins. Finally, the ileum, the last part of the small intestine, absorbs cholesterol, bile, salts, and vitamin B12.

By the time chyme has made its way to the end of the small intestine, the necessary nutrients have been absorbed into the bloodstream. What is left in the intestine is mostly waste, which will be handled by the next segment of the intestine, the large intestine.

4
The Wonderful World of Waste

At this point, your body has gotten what it needs from the food. Now the digestive system must get ready to expel what is left. In this chapter, we will examine the large intestine, which prepares and expels solid waste. Also, we will examine the urinary system, which is responsible for expelling liquid waste. Finally, there will be a discussion of digestive gases.

The Large Intestine

Chyme spends between one and four hours in the small intestine. This is after the two to four hours that the bolus spent in the stomach. Neither of these periods, however, is comparable to the amount of time substances stay in the large intestine. Materials usually spend around ten hours in the large intestine but can remain there for several days.

The large intestine, also called the colon, is a winding tube between three and five feet long. It winds up the right side of the body, across, and down the left side. It ends at the anus with the

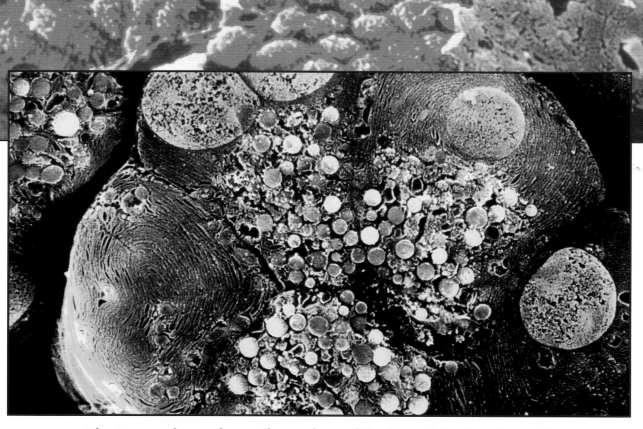

The image above shows the surface of the large intestine (magnification x800), a winding tube that prepares solid waste to be expelled.

anal sphincter, which controls the expulsion of solid waste.

Like the small intestine, the large intestine is divided into sections. The opening from the small intestine is called the ileocecal valve. This is where chyme passes from the ileum (the last part of the small intestine) into the cecum, the first section of the large intestine. The other sections of the large intestine are the ascending colon (which goes up on the right), the transversal colon (which goes across), the descending colon (which goes down on the left), and the sigmoid colon. The sigmoid colon leads into the rectum, the final part of the large intestine before the anus.

Attached to the cecum is an odd part of the large intestine: the appendix. The appendix is odd because no one knows what it does. Actually, the only time we really hear about it is when it gets infected. An inflamed appendix is a

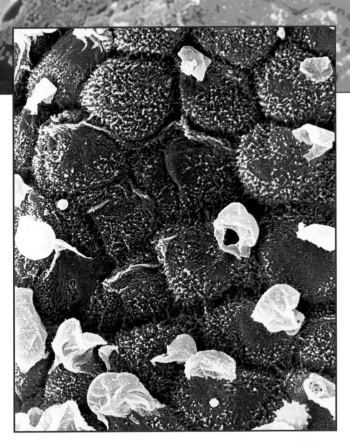

This is a close-up view of the mucosa, or lining, of the rectum. Feces move through the colon and collect in the rectum.

serious matter—the condition is known as appendicitis. When this happens, the appendix has to be surgically removed before it bursts. If the appendix bursts, the results can be fatal.

Unlike the appendix, however, much of the large intestine does have a very important function. The main function is to remove water from the chyme, now called feces, and prepare it for expulsion. You will remember that chyme is liquid. In contrast, feces are semisolid to solid.

If the large intestine isn't working properly, the feces remain in a liquid state. Feces move through the colon and collect in the rectum. When there is a sufficient amount of feces there, you feel the need to go to the bathroom—as in the common expression, "nature calls."

The Kidneys

The other time you need to go to the bathroom is to expel liquid waste, or urine. You might think that urine is part of the digestive system, too. Actually, it isn't. It's part of its own system.

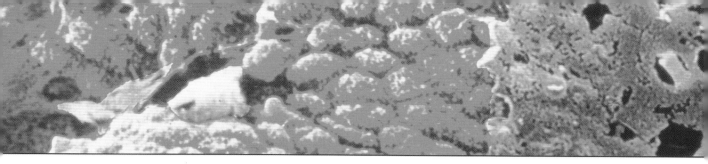

The waste that you expel when you urinate is the waste material from the entire body, picked up by the blood and brought to the urinary system. As you read in the previous chapter, blood picks up nutrients from the small intestine and delivers them to cells everywhere in the body. At the same time, blood also has to collect waste from the cells and get rid of it. This is the job of the kidneys.

Typically, the body has two working kidneys, one on each side, located near the small intestine. Blood flows to the kidneys via the renal artery. Inside the kidney are about one million filtering units called nephrons. The center of a nephron is called the glomerulus, and is made up of tiny blood vessels.

Located above the glomerulus is a clamplike structure called Bowman's capsule. Bowman's capsule applies pressure to filter the waste products from the blood. The waste products can include urea and uric acid, which are components of urine.

Blood is carried away from the kidney via the renal vein. Waste products travel down the ureter into the bladder, where they are stored until you go to the bathroom. When you go to the bathroom, you expel urine through the urethra.

You may notice that both solid waste feces and liquid waste urine don't always look the same. These differences are due to the varying composition of the waste. For solid foods, it can be a matter of what you ate—was the food fibrous, like leafy vegetables? It can also be a matter of how well your large intestines are working. Are they absorbing enough water from the feces?

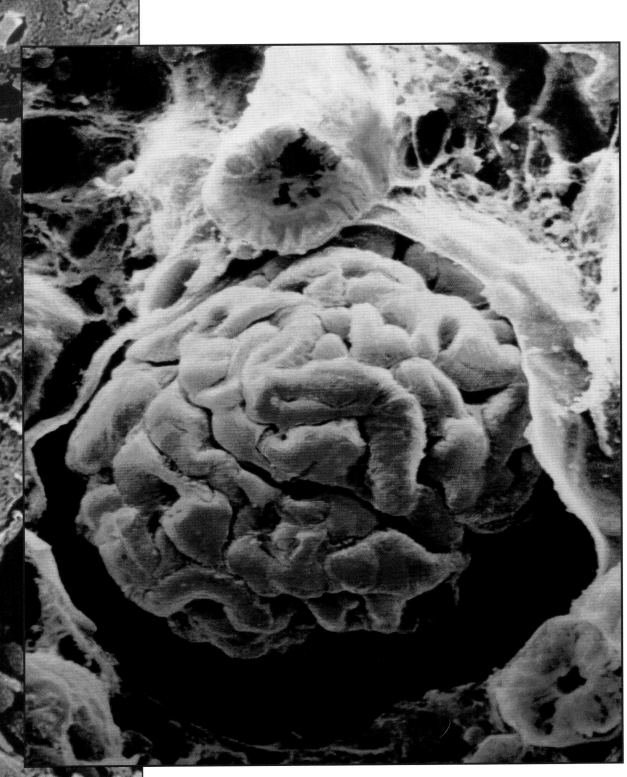

The kidneys absorb waste matter from the blood to be expelled in the urine.

For the kidneys, it is a matter of how much water your body can supply. If your body is running low on water, your kidneys will use less water in the urine. The result is urine that is a darker yellow. If the body has an overabundance of water, however, urine is lighter and can even be almost clear.

Digestion and Gas

For proper digestion to take place, several chemical reactions need to happen. As you know, the food you eat has to go through chemical reactions with enzymes and acids to be broken down into molecule-sized nutrients that can be transported by the blood. As a result of these chemical reactions, there is another waste product other than the feces that is made: gas.

Having gas is a natural and normal occurrence. Gas either is a byproduct of the chemical reactions that occur when the food we eat is broken down or is ingested with the food that we eat. Gas is categorized by whether it comes from the stomach and out of your mouth or whether it comes from the intestines.

Gases Part I: Belching

In some cultures, burping, or belching, is seen as a sign of appreciation for a well-prepared meal. Most times, however, belching is seen as a harmless social blunder that can be somewhat embarrassing.

Belching occurs because of gas trapped inside the stomach. Gas gets trapped in the stomach when we eat. If we eat quickly or talk while eating, we increase the risk of swallowing gas with our food. Also, if we eat certain foods that contain gases in them—carbonated drinks are an excellent example—gas will be released in our stomach as the acids and enzymes break the food down. Whipped foods that contain air are another example of foods that make us belch. Infants, because they are so new to the functions of breathing and eating, routinely get gas trapped in their stomach and need to be burped.

The best way to deal with gas in your stomach is to belch (of course, in a manner that is as socially acceptable as possible!). Sometimes when people cannot get air out of their stomach, they try to force the belch by swallowing more air (a common technique is to drink soda). The thought behind this is that by swallowing more air, such a large amount of air will build up that the body will need to release both the gas just swallowed and the gas already trapped inside the stomach.

What happens most often, however, is that more gas just winds up being trapped in the stomach. A better way to deal with stomach gas is to massage the stomach area gently. Also, ginger, like that found in ginger tea, is known to help soothe gas pain.

Gases Part II: Flatulence

The second type of gas is much more embarrassing and socially unacceptable—flatulence. Flatulence is the scientific (and proper!) term used when we pass intestinal gas (though we all know more unsavory terms for it).

This gas is predominately produced in the large intestine. There are 250 individual gases present, but the main components of flatulence are carbon dioxide, hydrogen, methane, nitrogen, and sulfur dioxide. These gases come from either the interactions of acidic compounds in the intestines or the reactions of bacteria inside the intestine.

None of these primary components, however, has any smell. It is other gases, like sulfide, that makes flatulence smell so bad.

Although flatulence is completely normal, if you suffer from excess flatulence you might want to monitor your intake of certain foods that produce gas. These foods include beans, artichokes, cabbage, onions, and green peppers.

FAMOUS FOR FLATULENCE

In the mid-1850s, Joseph Pujol was found to have an extraordinary talent. According to The Guinness Book of Records, he could carry a tune and imitate various noises with his flatulence. It was so peculiar that when he died scientists wanted to examine his body, but his family refused.

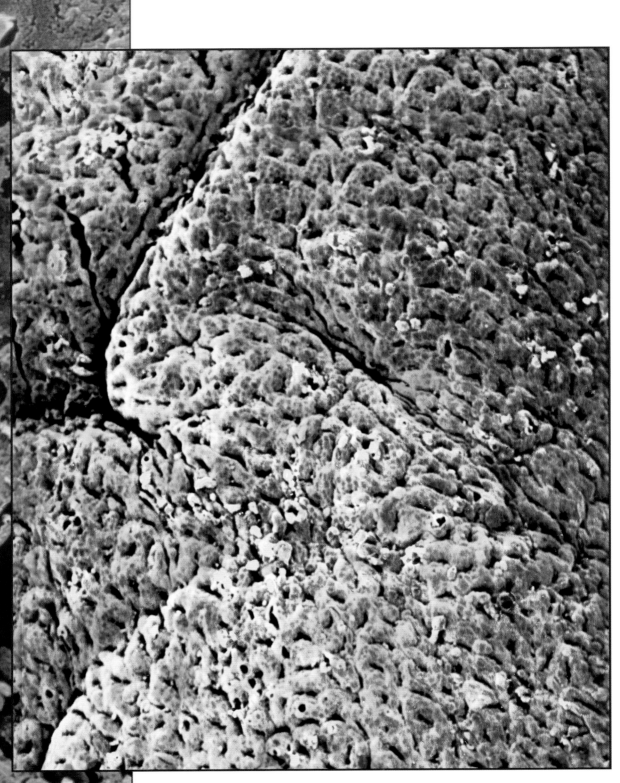

In the colon, undigestible food becomes feces with the absorption of excess water. This image (magnification x80) shows the glandular wall of the colon.

The Last Word on Waste

After waste is expelled, the digestive process is over. The foods that were eaten have been filtered of their valuable nutrients that help the body grow and function. The waste itself is useless to

> ## THE KIDNEYS THROUGHOUT YOUR LIFE
>
> Kidneys in adults weigh only about five ounces each. That's about a third of a pound. Amazingly, these small organs process about 425 gallons of blood each day. During the course of an average lifetime, the kidneys process about one million gallons of blood.

the body; however, waste from animals is often used to replenish soils that are low in nitrogen. Human waste, on the other hand, is usually flushed away.

Human waste is as natural as anything else, but most cultures find it repugnant. No one wants to talk about it, see it, or smell it, but it's simply a natural consequence of eating.

Our discussion of the functions of the digestive system ends here, with waste. The next chapter is a brief note on ways to keep your digestion healthy and avoid common digestive diseases.

5

Digestive Health

No discussion about the digestive system would be complete without some explanation of digestive health. As we've seen, the digestive system has many organs, all working together, each with very complicated jobs. Usually these organs work well together. In the first section of this chapter, we will find out different ways to keep our digestion healthy. In the section following, we will see what happens when the digestive system malfunctions.

Tips for Healthy Digestion

After having read how digestion happens, you can probably figure out what helps you maintain good digestion. The first two points should be obvious, and you've probably heard them before:

● Eat slowly. We often rush through meals, even though this can upset our digestive system. Eating quickly puts a strain on your digestive system. You may also wind up swallowing air,

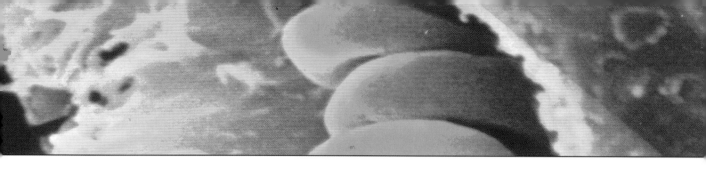

which can upset your stomach. Pace yourself and eat at a comfortable rate.

● Chew food well. The first step in breaking down your food is chewing. The better you chew, the less strain you put on your digestive system.

Other tips for healthy digestion build on what we've already discussed:

● Avoid swallowing air. For better digestion, you should avoid swallowing air as much as possible. You can do this by limiting the amount of carbonated beverages that you drink and by eating at a good, steady pace. Also, don't talk with your mouth full—not just because it's rude but also because it's bad for your digestion.

● Don't overeat. Overeating puts stress on your digestive system. Your stomach can expand quite a bit, but it shouldn't be expected to handle extreme volumes on a regular basis.

● Exercise. You've probably heard that exercise helps your body remain fit, but did you know that exercise also helps your digestion? When you exercise regularly, your body uses the materials prepared by your digestive system in an efficient way. Exercising is a great way to keep your digestive system balanced.

What Is "Eating Right"?

Many people are concerned about what they eat, but this doesn't mean that they know how to stay healthy. Sometimes people who want to lose weight end up starving themselves and not getting the nutrients they need. Other people are too busy to eat a proper meal and will eat whatever is at hand. Still other people are junk food addicts who love sweet, sticky, and fatty foods.

Obviously, none of these is advisable or healthy. You should also remain skeptical of any new, wonderful "diets." The most important thing is to be mindful of what you eat and to learn what a healthy diet means. For instance, you may have heard that fat and carbohydrates are "bad." If you are growing, though, you need plenty of fats and carbohydrates along with your proteins and vegetables. The key is to keep everything balanced and to eat fatty, sweet, or salty foods in moderation.

The best advice is to monitor what you eat and how you feel after eating it. If you feel ill after, say, eating an entire bag of greasy potato chips or an entire box of cookies, chances are that you shouldn't be eating so much at once. Also, notice if you have more or less energy and whether or not you feel weighed down after eating. Being mindful of what you eat is eating right.

Common Digestive Diseases

Like any organ system, the digestive system can sometimes suffer from diseases or serious problems in functioning. Some of these

diseases are fairly common—
we all experience a stomachache from time to time. Some
other diseases of the digestive system, however, are
quite extreme, and in some
cases even fatal.

Indigestion (Dyspepsia)

Basic indigestion, also called
dyspepsia, is the most common of digestive disorders.
This can include everything

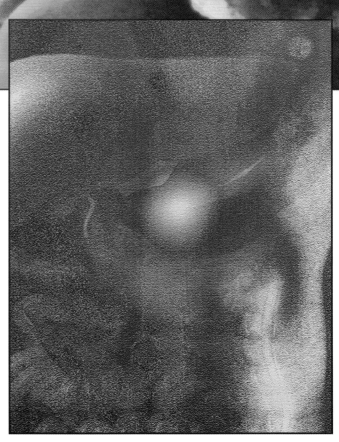

Heartburn, a form of indigestion, occurs when stomach acid moves back up into the esophagus.

from a stomachache to heartburn. Eating things that your stomach
might find disagreeable causes many stomachaches, but they can
also be caused by stress and by being upset. If you monitor what
you eat and eat properly, you can avoid most forms of dyspepsia.

One form of dyspepsia already mentioned (see chapter 2) is
heartburn. Although heartburn has nothing to do with the heart, it
does burn. Heartburn is the common term for when stomach acid
moves back up into the esophagus. Like other forms of dyspepsia,
heartburn can be controlled by monitoring what you eat. Also,
there are several medicines available that can combat heartburn
(you've probably seen commercials for them on television).

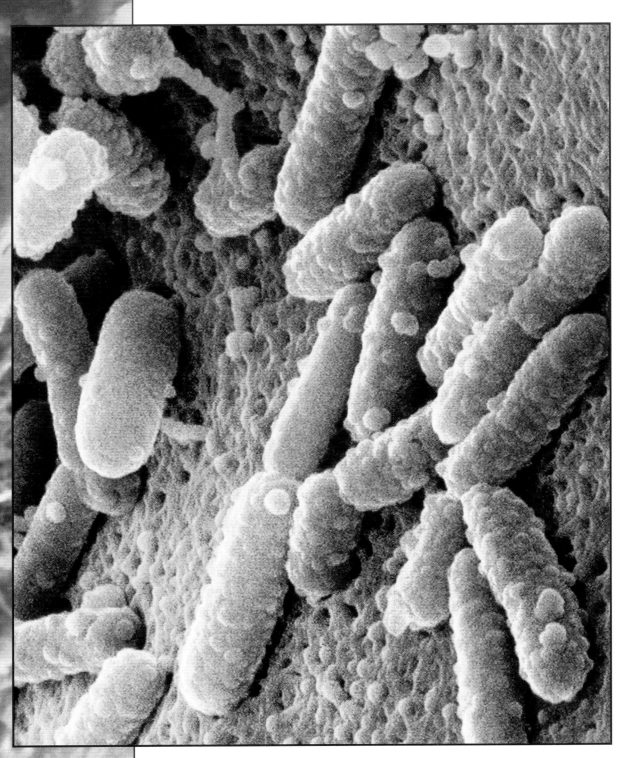

E. coli bacteria, which inhabit the intestines of humans and other animals, are usually harmless but may increase in number and cause problems such as diarrhea or urinary tract infections.

Diarrhea and Irritable Bowel Syndrome (IBS)

Diarrhea is not a disease in itself; rather, it is a symptom (a sign) of some other problem. This problem could be bacteria-related or it could be a symptom of irritable bowel syndrome (IBS).

IBS is a common disorder that affects the large intestine. In fact, it is the most common digestive complaint among adults. Symptoms can range from pain in the large intestine to inconsistent stool, or feces. It's often impossible to specify what causes IBS in a person because there are so many possible reasons. Some people think that the cause is psychological, while others think that it is related to diet. Some think that lactose intolerance (see below) is the underlying cause. Because there are so many things that can cause IBS, it is best treated on a case-by-case basis.

There are general guidelines, though, for treating IBS. The first is to monitor what you eat. Avoiding foods that cause excess gas and bowel irritation helps, as does eating a low-fat, high-fiber diet. Most cases of diarrhea stop after a day or so. There are also many medicines available that can stop this common problem. Chronic, or continuous, diarrhea, however, is cause for concern and should definitely be discussed with a doctor.

Lactose Intolerance

Over 50 million Americans suffer from lactose intolerance, which is a disorder where a person cannot digest lactose, a common part of

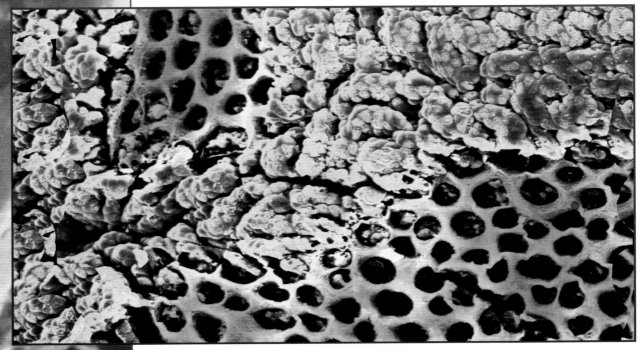

Ulcers, holes that form in the lining of the digestive system, are caused by bacteria.

most dairy products (including milk, cheese, and yogurt). Lactose intolerance occurs when the small intestine doesn't produce enough of the enzyme lactase, which breaks down milk sugars to be absorbed into the blood. When lactose cannot be absorbed into the blood, the effects can cause bloating, nausea, gas, and diarrhea.

Lactose intolerance is a cause for concern, but if an individual suffering from lactose intolerance carefully watches his or her diet, there should be no problems. Knowing what foods contain lactose—and avoiding them—is key for someone who is lactose intolerant. Even without most diary products, lactose-intolerant individuals can get their necessary calcium from other sources, such as tofu and spinach. There are also several products, such as soy and rice milk and soy cheese, that can be substituted for dairy products.

Ulcers

Ulcers are a tricky subject. Although ulcers are very serious, they are also more common than you might think. Ulcers are holes that form in the lining of your digestive system. Although ulcers can occur in any part of the system—from the esophagus to the intestines—they most often occur in the duodenum.

A common misunderstanding is that ulcers are caused by stress. This isn't really the case, however. Stress does affect the amount of acid that your digestive system produces, but ulcers are related to a particular bacterial infection. These bacteria (called *H. pylori*) cause the lining in the digestive walls to become very thin. As a result, the powerful enzymes and acids involved in the digestive system can break down the walls even further, eventually making a hole. Ulcers are typically treated with a combination of antibiotics that attack the infecting bacteria.

A Final Word on Digestion

The common remedies for most minor digestive disorders are to monitor what you eat and to eat well. After that, the digestive system will take care of itself. Like other internal systems in the body, the digestive system does its job without any extraordinary effort on our part. Knowing about our digestive system, however, helps us understand how important it is to help keep it running smoothly.

Glossary

bolus
Chewed food before it exits the stomach.

chyme
Partially digested food that has left the stomach and entered the small intestine.

duodenum
The first part of the small intestine.

epiglottis
Valve that covers the windpipe during swallowing.

ileum
Last part of the small intestine.

jejunum
Second part of the small intestine.

villi
Small fingerlike coils in the lining of the small intestine that allow nutrients to be passed into the blood.

For More Information

In the United States

American College of Gastroenterology (ACG)
4900 B South 31st Street
Arlington, VA 22206-1656
(703) 820-7400
Web site: http://www.acg.gi.org

The American Gastroenterological Association (AGA)
National Office
7910 Woodmont Avenue, Suite 700
Bethesda, MD 20814
(301) 654-2055
Web site: http://www.gastro.org

In Canada

Canadian Association of Gastroenterology
CAG National Office
28 Foster Crescent
Brampton, ON L6V 3M7
(905) 455-6289
Web site: http://www.gi.ucalgary.ca

Web Sites

About.com
http://kidshealth.about.com/kids/kidshealth/msub41.htm

Brainpop
http://www.brainpop.com/health/digestive

Innerbody.com
http://www.innerbody.com/htm/body.html

For Further Reading

Avraham, Regina. *The Digestive System*. Philadelphia: Chelsea House Publishers, 2000.

Ballard, Carol. *The Stomach and Digestive System*. Austin, TX: Raintree Steck-Vaughn Publishers, 1997.

———. *How Do We Taste and Smell?* Austin, TX: Raintree Steck-Vaughn Publishers, 1998.

Burnie, David. *The Concise Encyclopedia of the Human Body*. New York: DK Publishing, 1995.

Poole, Robert M. (ed.), *The Incredible Machine*. Washington, DC: National Geographic Society, 1995.

Silverstein, Alvin, Robert Silverstein, and Virginia Silverstein. *Digestive System*. New York: Twenty-First Century Books, 1994.

Index

A

acids, 13, 14, 20, 21, 30, 37, 41
amino acids, 8, 14, 21
amylase, 9, 14, 20, 21
anus, 24, 25
appendix, 25–26

B

bacteria, 14, 31, 39, 41
bile, 17, 18, 19, 21, 23
biliary system, 16–17
bladder, 27
blood/bloodstream, 5, 15, 16, 18, 20, 23, 27, 29, 33, 40
bolus, 10–11, 13, 16, 24

C

carbohydrates, 7, 8, 36
cecum, 25
chewing, 4, 8–10, 11, 35
chyme, 13, 15, 16, 17, 19, 20, 21, 23, 24, 25, 26

circulatory system, 5, 16
colon, 24, 25, 26

D

diarrhea, 39, 40
digestive health, 34–41
digestive system,
   definition of, 4
   diseases of, 36–41
   size of, 5
   tips for healthy digestion, 34–35
duodenum, 19, 21, 23, 41

E

endocrine system, 19, 20
energy, food as, 5, 7, 18, 21, 23, 36
enzymes, 9, 14, 19–20, 21, 29, 30, 40, 41
esophagus, 10–13, 37, 41
excretion, 4, 5, 10, 26

F

fats, 5, 7, 8, 13, 14, 17, 20, 21, 23, 36

feces, 26, 27, 29, 39
food, eating, 4, 5, 6–11, 13, 15, 16, 21,
  24, 27, 29–30, 31, 33, 34–36, 37,
  39, 40, 41

G
gall bladder, 18, 19, 21
gas, digestive, 24, 29–31, 39, 40
glucose, 18, 21

H
heart, 13, 16, 37
heartburn, 13, 37
hormones, 5, 19, 20
hydrochloric acid, 14–15

I
ileum, 21, 23, 25
indigestion, 37
irritable bowel syndrome, 39

J
jejunum, 21, 23

K
kidneys, 26–29, 33

L
lactose intolerance, 39–41
large intestine, 23, 24–26, 27, 31, 39
lipase, 14, 20, 21
liver, 16, 17, 21

M
mouth, 8–9, 10, 35

N
nutrients, 4, 5, 16, 23, 27, 29, 31, 36

P
pancreas, 19–20, 21
peptides, 14, 21
protein, 5, 7–8, 14, 20, 21, 36

R
rectum, 25, 36

S
saliva, 8, 9, 14
salivary glands, 8, 9, 14, 20
small intestine, 16, 17, 18, 19, 20–23,
  25, 27, 40
sphincters, 13, 15, 20, 24
starches, 7, 9, 20, 21
stomach, 11–15, 19, 20, 24, 29, 30,
  35, 37
sugars, 5, 7, 9, 18, 20, 21, 23, 40
swallowing, 8, 10, 30, 34–35

T
teeth, 8–9
tongue, 8, 9, 10

U
ulcers, 15, 41
urinary system, 24, 27
urine, 26–27, 29

W
waste, 5, 23, 24, 27, 29, 31–33
water, 15, 17, 19, 26, 27, 29

Credits

About the Author

Ben Morrison is a freelance writer and editor of college textbooks. He lives in New York.

Photo Credits

Pp. 5, 9, 17 © Life Art; p. 7 © Custom Medical; pp. 8, 25, 28 © Photo Researchers, Inc.; pp. 10, 14, 20, 26 © Quest/SPL/Photo Researchers, Inc.; p. 11 © Chemical Design LTD/SPL/Photo Researchers, Inc.; p. 12 © Professors P.M. Motta, K.R. Porter & P.M. Andrews/SPL/Photo Researchers, Inc.; pp. 18, 32, 40 © Prof. P. Motta/Dept. of Anatomy/University "La Sapienza," Rome/SPL/Photo Researchers, Inc.; p. 19 © Professors P. Motta & T. Naguro/SPL/Photo Researchers, Inc.; p. 22 © Meckes/Ottawa/Photo Researchers, Inc.; p. 25 © Oliver Meckes/Photo Researchers, Inc.; p. 37 © David Gifford/SPL/Photo Researchers, Inc.; p. 38 © Andrew Syred/SPL/Photo Researchers, Inc.
Cover, Front Matter, Back Matter © Prof. P. Motta/Dept. of Anatomy/University "La Sapienza", Rome/SPL/Photo Researchers, Inc.
Ch. 1 © CNRI/SPL/Custom Medical: mucosa of the stomach.
Ch. 2 © Prof. P. Motta/G. Franchitto/University "La Sapienze," Rome/SPL/Photo Researchers, Inc.: filiform papillae on the dorsal surface of the tongue.
Ch. 3 © Prof. P. Motta/Dept. of Anatomy/University "La Sapienze," Rome/SPL/Photo Researchers, Inc.: section through the duodenum.
Ch. 4 © Quest/SPL/Photo Researchers, Inc.:large intestine mucosa.
Ch. 5 © Prof. P. Motta/Dept. of Anatomy/University "La Sapienze," Rome/SPL/Photo Researchers, Inc.: liver cells.

Layout

Geri Giordano

Series Design

Cindy Williamson

FIELDS CORNER

BAKER & TAYLOR